The Quest FOR Comfort

~ THE STORY OF ~
THE HEIDELBERG CATECHISM

BY WILLIAM BOEKESTEIN | ILLUSTRATED BY EVAN HUGHES

RHB | REFORMATION HERITAGE BOOKS

Grand Rapids, Michigan

The Quest for Comfort: The Story of the Heidelberg Catechism
© 2011 by William Boekestein

Reformation Heritage Books
2965 Leonard St. NE
Grand Rapids, MI 49525
616-977-0889 / Fax 616-285-3246
orders@heritagebooks.org
www.heritagebooks.org

Library of Congress Cataloging-in-Publication Data

Boekestein, William.
 The quest for comfort : the story of the Heidelberg catechism / by William Boekestein ; illustrated by Evan Hughes.
     p. cm.
 ISBN 978-1-60178-152-9 (harcover : alk. paper)
 1. Heidelberger Katechismus--Juvenile literature. 2. Friedrich III, Elector Palatine, 1515-1576--Juvenile literature. 3. Olevian, Caspar, 1536-1587--Juvenile literature. 4. Ursinus, Zacharias, 1534-1583--Juvenile literature. I. Hughes, Evan. II. Title.
 BX9428.B625 2011
 238'.42--dc23
                                        2011033845

For additional Reformed literature, both new and used, request a free book list from Reformation Heritage Books at the above regular or e-mail address.

Printed in the United States of America
11 12 13 14 15 16/10 9 8 7 6 5 4 3 2 1

When was the last time you felt bad? Maybe you were very sick. Maybe you did something wrong. Maybe you were lonely or scared.

In times like these we need comfort. We need to know that despite our problems and our sin, God is on our side, working out everything for our good.

Many years ago God used three men to write a little book that explained the only true comfort in life and in death.

These men lived in a time when comfort was badly needed. Most people believed they could have comfort in this life only when they were good. Even if they believed they were good, they had very little comfort about what would happen to them after they died. Few knew the real and lasting comfort that God promises through His Word. That's why these three men wrote their little book.

The three men were Caspar Olevianus, Zacharias Ursinus, and Frederick III. The little book they wrote, with God's help, is called the Heidelberg Catechism.

Frederick III   Zacharias Ursinus   Caspar Olevianus

As a young man, Caspar Olevianus thought he was going to be a lawyer. He went to school in France and studied hard. But he also found time to play.

One day he was relaxing along a river with some fellow students. Some of the students decided to get drunk and fool around with a rowboat in the river. While Caspar looked on, the boat flipped upside down, and the students began to drown.

Caspar and others dove in and rescued all of the young men, except one. Herman Louis, the son of Frederick III, was drowned. Then and there Caspar decided to become a minister after he finished his studies in law.

Like many other Protestants of his day, Caspar began his training for the ministry in Geneva, Switzerland, under the teaching of John Calvin.

After his training he returned to his hometown of Treves, Germany, to teach philosophy and Latin. He also began to preach. Caspar's goal was for the church to be reformed according to the Word of God. So he plainly and powerfully preached what the Bible taught. He also told about some of the errors of the Roman Catholic Church.

Angered by his preaching, Roman Catholic leaders ordered him to stop and leave the city. He refused, giving the same answer that Peter and the apostles gave fifteen hundred years earlier: "We ought to obey God rather than men" (Acts 5:29).

Within a month, Caspar's opponents sent 120 horsemen to crush the Reformation in Treves. Caspar and twelve others were arrested and thrown into prison.

News of Caspar's arrest reached Frederick III, the father of Herman Louis, whom Caspar had tried to save from drowning. In God's providence, Frederick III had recently become the elector, or ruler, of a German state called the Palatinate. Being friendly to the Protestant cause, Frederick used his position to purchase Caspar's freedom. He also gave him an invitation: "Come to the city of Heidelberg to teach and preach."

At the age of twenty-four, Caspar accepted his offer and became a theological professor and pastor of the Holy Ghost Church in Heidelberg, Germany.

Caspar was not the only one about to make a new start in Heidelberg. Zacharias Ursinus, who was two years older than Caspar, had received a similar offer from the new elector. "I would like you to be the principal of the College of Wisdom, Heidelberg's theological seminary," wrote Frederick.

Zacharias had been preaching for several years under very difficult circumstances in his hometown of Breslau, in modern-day Poland. He was a calm and shy person. The people of his congregation were not calm like Zacharias, but were often rude to their pastor.

One of Zacharias's best friends was a man who shared his quiet personality. Philip Melanchthon (the assistant of the bold Martin Luther) and Zacharias had been friends and traveling companions ever since Zacharias had studied with Philip at the University of Wittenberg.

Right in the middle of Zacharias's difficult church situation, his dear friend Philip died. The pressures of pastoring in Breslau became too much to bear. Zacharias fled to Zurich, Switzerland, to seek relief. While studying in Zurich, Zacharias received a letter carrying the seal of the elector of Heidelberg.

Zacharias was eager to teach the Bible in a fresh setting. On the other hand, he had been looking forward to living a quiet, peaceful life out of the center of attention. Still, he accepted Frederick's invitation and moved to Heidelberg.

Frederick had become the ruler of the lands surrounding Heidelberg for only a few years before Caspar and Zacharias arrived. But God had been preparing him his entire life for the challenges he was about to face.

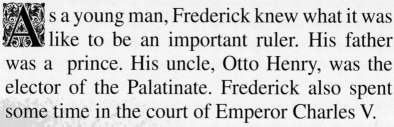

As a young man, Frederick knew what it was like to be an important ruler. His father was a prince. His uncle, Otto Henry, was the elector of the Palatinate. Frederick also spent some time in the court of Emperor Charles V.

He could not help noticing that some of the leaders did not use their positions for good. Instead, they used their power to live for pleasure. He may have wondered how he would live if he were given an opportunity to rule.

The Lord used a wonderful young woman to test Frederick's question. Frederick fell in love with a German princess named Maria. Maria loved the Bible and the writings of the Reformers and would not marry a man who didn't share her passion for God. At Maria's challenge, Frederick began to study Bible teaching.

In God's timing Frederick and Maria were married, and in their castle home they raised seven children.

During their parenting years, this godly couple learned their need for comfort both in life and in death. Besides losing their son Herman to drowning, one of their daughters died when she was only fourteen.

When Frederick was forty-four years old, he received news of the death of another family member. His Uncle Otto had died childless. This meant that Frederick was the new elector of the Palatinate.

And what a time to begin leading his people! For generations most people had belonged to the Roman Catholic Church. Many Roman Catholics simply accepted what their leaders taught them; they didn't know from their own study and experience what the Bible said.

Almost fifty years earlier Martin Luther had helped begin a reformation of doctrine and life. After him, others like John Calvin and Ulrich Zwingli had encouraged further reformation. Many of the changes were good, but change can make people uneasy. Things had gotten so bad in Heidelberg that a minister and a deacon had recently started a fist fight in the middle of a worship service over disagreements about the Lord's Supper!

Frederick desperately wanted to bring peace to his land. He also wanted to teach his people, in a simple way, what the Bible really says. He couldn't do this himself. He would need help.

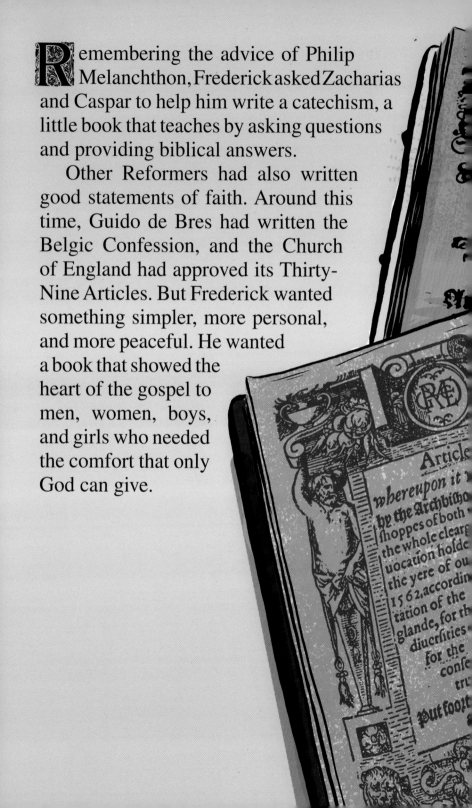

Remembering the advice of Philip Melanchthon, Frederick asked Zacharias and Caspar to help him write a catechism, a little book that teaches by asking questions and providing biblical answers.

Other Reformers had also written good statements of faith. Around this time, Guido de Bres had written the Belgic Confession, and the Church of England had approved its Thirty-Nine Articles. But Frederick wanted something simpler, more personal, and more peaceful. He wanted a book that showed the heart of the gospel to men, women, boys, and girls who needed the comfort that only God can give.

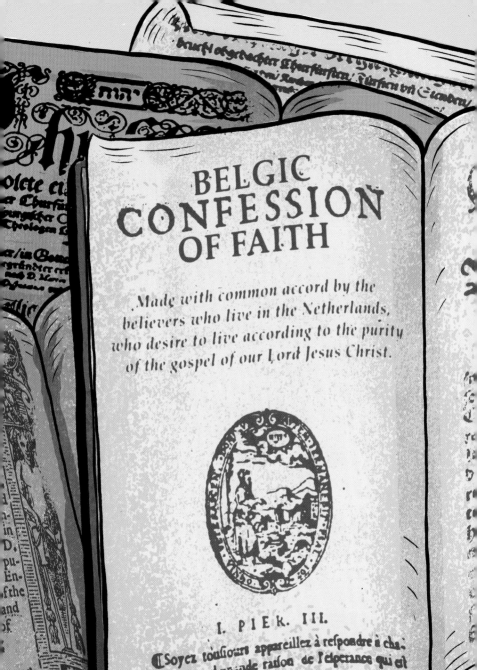

BELGIC CONFESSION OF FAITH

Made with common accord by the
believers who live in the Netherlands,
who desire to live according to the purity
of the gospel of our Lord Jesus Christ.

I. PIER. III.

Soyez tousiours appareillez à respondre à cha-
cun qui vous demande raison de l'esperance qui est
en vous.

The first question and answer of the new catechism is still one of the most treasured examples of Christian writing ever produced:

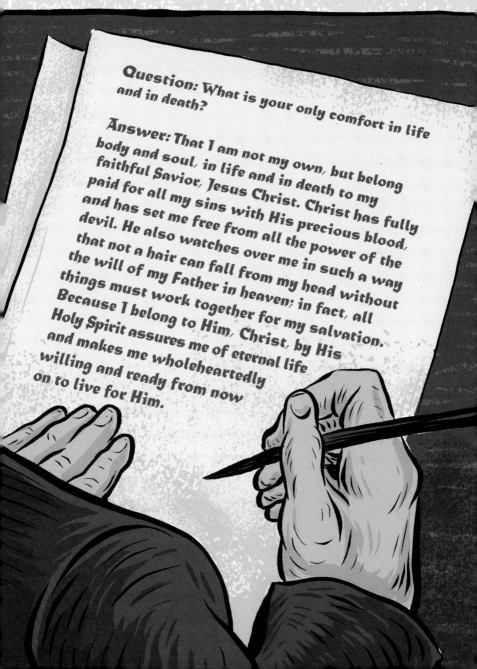

Question: What is your only comfort in life and in death?

Answer: That I am not my own, but belong body and soul, in life and in death to my faithful Savior, Jesus Christ. Christ has fully paid for all my sins with His precious blood, and has set me free from all the power of the devil. He also watches over me in such a way that not a hair can fall from my head without the will of my Father in heaven; in fact, all things must work together for my salvation. Because I belong to Him, Christ, by His Holy Spirit assures me of eternal life and makes me wholeheartedly willing and ready from now on to live for Him.

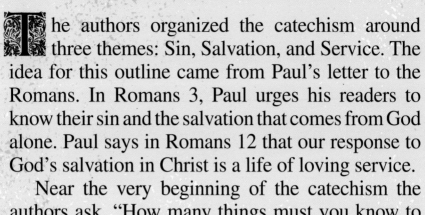

The authors organized the catechism around three themes: Sin, Salvation, and Service. The idea for this outline came from Paul's letter to the Romans. In Romans 3, Paul urges his readers to know their sin and the salvation that comes from God alone. Paul says in Romans 12 that our response to God's salvation in Christ is a life of loving service.

Near the very beginning of the catechism the authors ask, "How many things must you know to live and die in the joy of true and lasting comfort?" With this question they encourage their readers to begin a quest for the comfort that only God can give.

2 *Salvation*

The young men Frederick had enlisted to help him had written just the book he was hoping for. Others liked it as well. Just a few months after it was finished, John Calvin called Frederick the "most illustrious prince" and applauded his "labor to cherish and promote true religion."

After having other teachers and pastors inspect his little book and adding a few thoughts of his own, Frederick sent it to the printing press in 1563.

The catechism became hugely popular almost overnight. So many people wanted a copy of this "book of comfort" that three times in the first year, more had to be printed. Besides the Bible, only two other books have been as widely read as the Heidelberg Catechism.

But not everyone was pleased with Frederick and his catechism. He was accused with many serious, false charges. In 1566 he was allowed to defend himself at the Diet (or Meeting) of Augsburg. At Augsburg dozens of important rulers were asked to decide if Frederick should be punished for his book. He could lose his crown—or maybe his life!

At first the outcome looked very bad. After Frederick was allowed to speak, however, most people were so impressed by his godliness that even his enemies began calling him Frederick the Pious (or Godly). Frederick certainly deserved this title. There have been few rulers before or since who have modeled such godliness.

adly, within a few short years, Frederick died. Upon his death, his son Louis became the new ruler in the Palatinate. Louis hated his father's catechism. He banned its use and banished from the land over six hundred Reformed teachers and preachers.

After leaving Heidelberg, Zacharias preached and taught in a neighboring German territory under the protection of Frederick's second son, Casimir. When Louis died after ruling only six years, Casimir honored his father's legacy by reintroducing the catechism to his city. Caspar spent his last years helping to organize the Reformed church in another part of Germany.

Within eleven years of Frederick's death, both Zacharias and Caspar had also passed into glory. But their precious little "book of comfort" remains a lasting tribute to the gospel of their Lord and Savior, Jesus Christ.

"Are you serious—a children's book about the composition of a dry, pedagogical, theological document?" Good question!

But this is no ordinary document, and the record of its birth is anything but boring. The Heidelberg Catechism represents a rarely equaled blend of doctrine and piety. Historian Philip Schaff said that the catechism "is the product of the heart as well as the head, full of faith and unction from above. It is fresh, lively, glowing, yet clear, sober, self-sustained. The ideas are biblical and orthodox, and well fortified by apt Scripture proofs…. Altogether, the Heidelberg Catechism is more than a book, it is an institution, and will live as long as the Reformed Church." For this reason it remains the most influential of all the Reformation catechisms. The three primary men who helped write it were believers who were driven by devotion and conviction. They teach us that deeply held beliefs and profound theological truths are worthy of the difficulties often faced defending them.

The question may still be asked, "Why should our children care about a catechism and its history?" In the first place, the catechism was written for them. Its authors knew that the hearts of children are both tender and absorbent. Additionally, many children grow up memorizing the catechism (or one like it) or at least hearing it preached. It is only reasonable that they should understand and appreciate its background.

The basic themes of the Heidelberg Catechism are as simple as the gospel it explains. Because we are sinners (Rom. 3:19–20), we need a righteousness that comes from God. Because God freely gives this righteousness to His children (Rom. 3:21–24), we need to live lives of loving gratitude (Rom. 12:1). Impart these themes to your children—and to yourself! There is no better time to teach people the foundations of the faith than when they are young.

Those interested in further reading on the history and doctrine of the Heidelberg Catechism are encouraged to read Thea Van Halsema's *Three Men Came to Heidelberg and Glorious Heretic: The Story of Guido de Bres* (Grand Rapids: I.D.E.A. Ministries, 1996). More advanced readers will appreciate any of the many devotional commentaries on the catechism. Two of this author's favorites are Kevin DeYoung, *The Good News We Almost Forgot* (Chicago: Moody, 2010) and G. I. Williamson, *The Heidelberg Catechism: A Study Guide* (Phillipsburg, N.J.: P&R, 1993).